Job *Search*

Carol Staudacher
and
Susan M. Freese

LIFE SKILLS HANDBOOKS

CENTURY

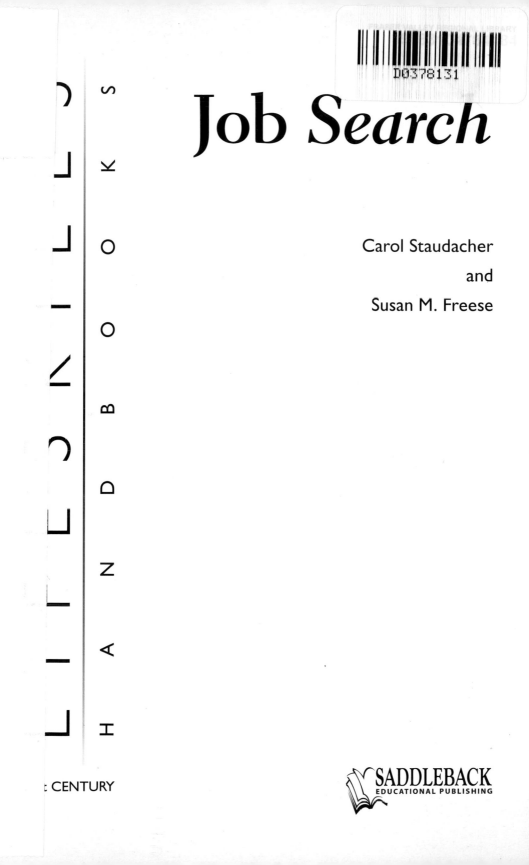

SADDLEBACK
EDUCATIONAL PUBLISHING

ISBN-13: 978-1-61651-658-1
ISBN-10: 1-61651-658-5
eBook: 978-1-61247-346-8

Printed in Guangzhou, China
1111/CA21101811

16 15 14 13 12   1 2 3 4 5

Contents

Workplace Readiness

Getting your first job is a huge step toward becoming independent. But how do you know what job is right for you? What kind of work are you interested in? How much money will you make? And what job benefits will be provided? Learning about all these topics will make you ready for the workplace—now and in the future.

Planning for a Bright Future

Maura wasn't surprised when her high school guidance counselor told her she should be a veterinarian. That was the career recommended by a test she'd taken. The test was about personal interests and possible careers. But Maura had known long before taking the test that she'd like to work with animals.

Becoming a veterinarian would mean going to college for about 10 years. Maura had learned about the educational requirements by reading online. She'd also learned about where vets work and what kinds of things they do. Wanting to know more, Maura visited several area animal clinics. She learned a lot by talking to the doctors about their work.

Ten years was a long time, for sure! But Maura had a plan for how to become a vet. She'd gotten a job in one of the clinics she visited. She planned to work there the summer after high school and then during college. She would start attending college at the local university. But to go to veterinary school,

she would have to move out of state. Getting good grades in her early college years would help her get into vet school. And having experience working in an animal clinic would help her get another part-time job after she moved.

Maura's plan covered both her education and her work experience. She was sure that following that plan would help her reach her goal of becoming a veterinarian.

CHAPTER 1

Aptitude Tests and Interest Inventories

In the world of work, you have many different job choices. But what kind of job will be best for you? Which **trade** or **profession** will give you the most satisfaction? Which **occupation** will best match your skills and interests?

Trade	Profession	Occupation
A job that requires skill in work done by hand or using machines. Examples include electrician, carpenter, machinist, and plumber.	A job that requires knowledge and skills developed through formal education and training. Examples include accountant, teacher, lawyer, and doctor.	A person's main job or usual business. Most people earn their living through their occupation.

Learning About Your Skills and Interests

You can learn the answers to these questions by taking two kinds of tests:

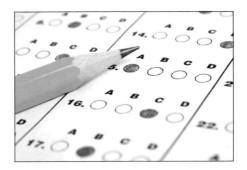

→ **Aptitude tests:** The word *aptitude* means "skill" or "ability." An aptitude test helps determine what you're good at. This kind of test isn't like a math or history exam. It's often given on a computer with special software or on a special Web site. The questions on an aptitude test are designed to discover your natural abilities. They're also designed to see how quickly or easily you figure things out or learn new information.

→ **Interest inventories:** An inventory is a survey or checklist. An *interest inventory* might ask you to read a list of activities and check the ones you'd like to do. After you answer all the items, you'll get an evaluation of your answers. It will suggest kinds of jobs that seem right for you. For instance, it might tell you that you should work outdoors or that you like to help people.

[FACT]

Types of Aptitude Tests

As many as 5,000 different aptitude tests are available. All of them evaluate one or more of the following areas:

1. **Verbal ability:** How well you communicate
2. **Numeric ability:** How well you do basic math
3. **Abstract reasoning:** How well you understand complex concepts and solve problems
4. **Spatial ability:** How well you mentally work with shapes
5. **Mechanical ability:** How well you understand mechanics and engineering
6. **Data checking:** How well you find errors in numbers and other detailed information

Sample Questions

Here are some questions similar to those you might find on an aptitude test:

1. DeShawn is shorter than Dan. Devon is shorter than DeShawn. Who is the shortest of the three?
   a. DeShawn
   b. Dan
   c. Devon
   d. None of the above

2. What number should come next in this series: 1 1 2 3 5 ?
   a. 7
   b. 10
   c. 8
   d. 9

3. *Lake* is to *puddle* as *wide* is to
   a. river
   b. short
   c. narrow
   d. tiny

4. Which word should come first alphabetically?
   a. bland
   b. blame
   c. bran
   d. blank

Here are some questions like those you might find on an interest inventory:

1. Which would you rather do?
   - ☐ work with people
   - ☐ work with machines

2. Where would you prefer to work?
   - ☐ indoors
   - ☐ outdoors

3. Which of the following do you most enjoy?
   - ☐ watching sports on TV
   - ☐ reading a book

4. When you are feeling sad, what would you rather do?
   - ☐ be by yourself
   - ☐ be with other people

Taking Aptitude Tests and Interest Inventories

School guidance counselors can usually give various kinds of aptitude tests and interest inventories. Your counselor can interpret your answers and help you decide which careers you might look into.

Also check the library for books about aptitude tests and interest inventories. Look for explanations of how they work. You can find these tests and inventories online, too. If you want to, you can test yourself. Then you can match your results with different job types and career categories.

No matter how you go about it, exploring your aptitudes and interests is an important first step in a job search.

Uses of Aptitude Tests

According to the American Management Association, 70% of US employers use some kind of skills test. One of the most common uses of these tests is to review job applicants. For most jobs, employers test applicants in at least basic math and language skills. For some jobs, specific skills tests are given, too. For example, suppose you're applying for a job in engineering or electronics. You would likely be given a test of mechanical ability.

Preparing for an Aptitude Test

It would be difficult to prepare for an aptitude test by studying all the material it might cover. You can prepare, though, by understanding what the test will be like:

- **Multiple-choice questions:** Most aptitude tests ask multiple-choice questions. To get credit for a question, you must select the correct answer from among several choices.

- **Strictly timed format:** Most aptitude tests follow specific time requirements. A typical test might allow you 30 minutes to complete 30 questions.

- **Exam conditions:** Some aptitude tests must be taken on paper at a testing center. Others can be taken online from home or work.

CHAPTER 2

Career Categories and Preparation

What are you good at? Knowing your aptitudes can be very helpful in choosing a career. And what do you like? Knowing your interests can be helpful, too.

So, what type of career looks good to you?

Popular Career Categories

→ **Sales:** Sales people in the computer industry sell *hardware* or *software.* Real estate agents sell buildings and land. Store clerks sell items ranging from clothing to auto parts.

Categories

Groups or types. Items are placed into categories based on their similarities.

Computer hardware

The mechanical and electronic parts of a computer.

Computer software

The directions and data that make the computer work. Computer software is sometimes referred to as *programs* or *applications*.

→ **Construction:** Careers in which people build things include carpenter, sheet metal worker, electrician, mason, and plumber.

→ **Manufacturing:** People who work in factories make cars, clothing, appliances, and more.

→ **Clerical:** Clerical workers provide help in offices and similar settings. Positions include administrative assistant, court reporter, and customer service representative.

→ **Government:** Government employees serve the community in roles such as firefighter, police officer, postal worker, and urban planner.

→ **Environment:** So-called green jobs include *sustainable* farmer, solar power installer, lab technician, and home energy analyst.

Sustainable
Describes something that has minimal long-term effects on the environment.

→ **Professions:** Professional careers include teacher, nurse, social worker, accountant, lawyer, and doctor.

Of course, there are many more career categories and jobs than are listed here. Check out Web sites such as the one from the Bureau of Labor Statistics. Use these sites to help you match your aptitudes and interests with job ideas.

[FACT]

The Bureau of Labor Statistics

The Bureau of Labor Statistics (BLS) is part of the US government. The BLS gathers and publishes information about a wide range of work-related topics. For job seekers, the most useful part of the BLS Web site is called "Occupations." Go to www.bls.gov/bls/occupation.htm. There, you'll find detailed information about specific occupations:

- The education and training needed
- The kinds of tasks or activities involved
- The environment in which the work is done
- The current number of jobs
- Future estimates of available jobs
- The earnings and working conditions

Preparing for a Career

Suppose you've picked a job that matches your talents and interests. Now, you need to find out what kinds of education or training are required for the job. For example, to do some sales jobs, you don't need anything more than a high school diploma. But what about other jobs?

→ To be an electrician, you'll need to get training at a special school. Then, you'll need to work closely under someone else's supervision for a period of time.

→ To be a postal worker, you must have a high school diploma or GED. You must also pass a government service exam.

→ If you're interested in being a police officer, you have to graduate from high school. Then, you have to take criminal justice classes at a college or university and go to the police academy. (The requirements vary by city and state.)

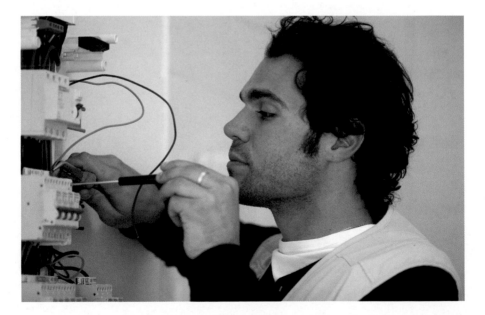

→ If you want to be a lawyer, you'll need to go to a university and earn several degrees. After that, you'll have to take a test and get a license to practice law.

Sometimes, the first career idea you have isn't the right one for you. So, you'll want to explore several possibilities. But you'll be off to a very good start if you stay in school and build your skills. Soon, you'll be looking forward to your first day on the job!

Getting a GED

The GED is a test of General Educational Development. It's usually taken by someone who didn't graduate from high school. Passing the test shows that the individual has basic knowledge. Five areas are tested: language arts, social studies, math, science, and writing. To take the test, the individual can't currently be enrolled in high school. He or she must also be at least 16 years old. Some testing centers charge a fee for taking the GED test, but others give it for free. Information about taking the GED test is usually available from the local public school system.

CHAPTER 3

Salaries, Wages, and Job Benefits

What should you think about when you're considering a job? Two things are extremely important: how much you'll get paid and what benefits you'll be provided.

Getting Paid

Workers in different careers are usually paid in different ways. People working in the professions and many office-type jobs usually get paid a *salary.* People working in the trades and in manufacturing jobs usually get paid *wages.*

Salary

A payment that's made to a worker for a set amount of money. It's paid on a regular basis, such as every two weeks.

Wages

A payment that's made to a worker for each hour or piece of work he or she completes. It's also paid on a regular basis, such as every two weeks.

Receiving Benefits

Job benefits are another key thing to consider before taking a job. Benefits usually include things such as paid vacation, sick leave, and health insurance. Other benefits might be the use of a company car, receiving company stock, or getting a discount on products the company sells.

$$$ Insurance $$$ Sick Days $$$ $$$ Vacation $$$ $$$ Savings Plans

[FACT]

Facts about Employee Benefits

- **Average number of paid holidays:** 10
- **Average number of vacation days:** 9.4 (after one year of employment)
- **Employers that offer some kind of pension plan:** Almost 50%
- **Employers that offer health insurance:** Approximately 75% (but many require employees to pay for part of it)
- **Employers that believe benefits attract employees:** 65%
- **Benefits offered by companies rated the best places to work:** Health club memberships, onsite day care, and education cost reimbursement
- **Employees' most desired "perks," or small extras provided by employers:** Flexible schedules and casual dress

After working many years, you may receive a *pension* from your employer. A pension provides income to live on after you retire.

Having good benefits is like getting paid extra. Think about what it would cost if you had

Pension
Money and other benefits provided to a retired employee by the company he or she worked for.

to pay for these things on your own. For example, health insurance is expensive to buy on your own. Many people can't afford it at all. What happens if they have an accident or illness? They must pay for all of their doctor visits, lab tests, hospital stays, and medications.

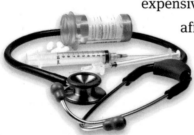

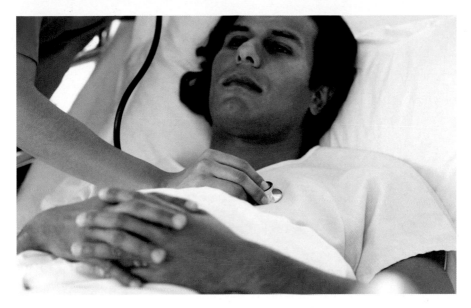

That's why health insurance is such an important job benefit. Having it could save you thousands of dollars. You might think about accepting a lower salary rather than take a job that doesn't provide health insurance.

[FACT]

Buying Your Own Health Insurance

- More than 26.5 million Americans are covered by health insurance plans they pay for themselves.
- The average amount they pay each year is $2,985 for a single person and $6,328 for a family.
- The cost varies greatly from state to state. For example, in New York, the average cost for a family is $13,296. But in Iowa, the same insurance plan costs $5,609.

The Whole Package

Be sure to look at the whole package
when considering a job. First, figure
out how much money you'll need each
month. Add up what you pay for housing,
food, transportation, insurance, and other
basic expenses. This amount is your *cost of
living*. Second, look at how much income
you'll have from your job and what benefits
are included.

When Jessica graduated from high school, she was offered a job in
the office of a large automobile repair business. She knew she would
learn a lot there. She would have a variety of duties, and she liked the
people she met at her interview.

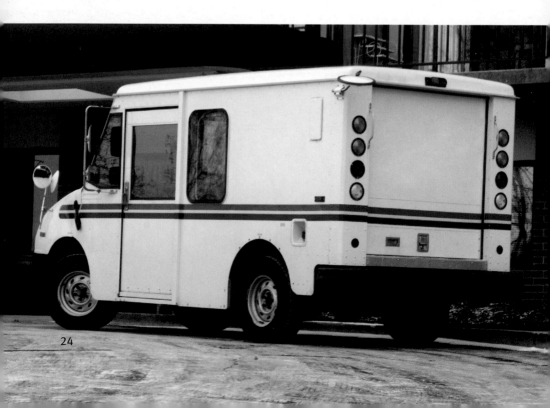

Jessica had also taken the test required to get a job at the post office. She was offered a position there, too. A lot of that job involved working by herself, at least at first. She would also have to work some odd hours and weekends.

Jessica was surprised when she compared the two jobs' salaries and benefits. The salaries were nearly the same. But the post office job offered much better benefits.

After thinking it over, Jessica decided that the post office job was the best choice. Having good benefits was important for her long-time financial security.

[FACT]

Comparing Costs of Living

The cost of living varies greatly from one US city to another. If you're planning to move, you should figure out how much it will cost to live at your new location. For example, suppose that now, you live in Denver, Colorado, and you earn $30,000 a year. If you move to San Francisco, California, you'll have to earn $47,662 to have the same standard of living. To make your own comparison of cities, search online for "cost of living calculators."

CHAPTER 4

Short-Term and Long-Term Goals

Some jobs don't really lead anywhere. They pay enough to cover your bills, but that's about it. They clearly aren't the first step on a career path.

Other jobs are more challenging. They offer lots of opportunities to learn. These jobs lead to career *advancement.*

Advancement

Improving and making progress in a job. Signs of advancement include being promoted to a higher position and having greater responsibilities. Other signs include earning more money and getting better benefits.

Being Happy with What He Has

Shane has a job that he enjoys most of the time. He's a cab driver. He knows his job will never change much—no matter how many years he does it. In 10 years, he'll still be bringing people to the airport, taking tourists to restaurants, and driving senior citizens to the market. But he doesn't mind. He likes driving and meeting people.

Shane's goal is simply to make a living. He isn't eager to learn new things or to develop new skills. He earns a salary and tips, but he doesn't have any chance for advancement. He isn't moving toward a higher-paid position with more interesting responsibilities.

[FACT]

Changing Jobs

- On average, people stay in their jobs 4.1 years.
- Older people (ages 55 to 64) stay in their jobs 9.9 years.
- Younger people (ages 25 to 34) stay in their jobs 2.7 years.
- Most workers have 10.8 different jobs between the ages of 18 and 42.
- Most people change jobs more often in their teens and early twenties than in their thirties.

Looking to the Future

Erin loves working with young children. She works as an assistant at a preschool. Every morning, she helps the teacher take care of the children. And every afternoon, she takes classes at the university. She also takes a class one night a week.

Erin's **long-term goal** is to be a kindergarten teacher. She knows that it will take a lot of time and patience to achieve her goal. But she's steadily gaining both education and experience. For now, she enjoys planning for the future. One day, she may even teach other people how to work with children.

Long-term goal

Something to be achieved in a longer time period, such as several years or even a lifetime. At work, a long-term goal might be to own your own business.

Erin's current job is an important step toward her long-term goal. She looks forward to advancing in her career. She's working her way up in the teaching profession.

Guidelines for Goal Setting

1. Make sure the goal is something you want, not something others want.
2. Determine how achieving the goal will benefit you.
3. Think about how the goal fits with your values and other goals.
4. Write down the goal, and describe in detail what you want to do.
5. Create a plan for achieving the goal. Break it into specific steps.
6. Set a time frame in which you will achieve the goal.

Having a Dream

Even as a child, P. J. was fascinated by the restaurant business. Whenever he got a chance, he tasted different foods and checked out what was happening in the kitchen.

When P. J. graduated from high school, his ***short-term goal*** was to earn enough money to live on his own. So, he got a job as a waiter in a small, medium-priced restaurant. After six months, he became a waiter in a nicer restaurant. He also started to attend cooking school at the nearby community college. Now, his long-term goal is to become a master chef. A master chef creates the restaurant's menu and supervises all the work of cooking and presenting the food.

P. J. is enjoying learning all about restaurants. He's happy to watch, listen, and learn while he advances in his career.

Short-term goal

Something to be achieved in the near future, from one month up to one year. At work, a short-term goal might be to get a raise or promotion.

Qualities of Good Goals

1. **Measureable:** How will you determine if you're making progress toward your goal? Find ways to measure your effort and achievement.

2. **Meaningful:** Why is achieving this goal important? You'll be more likely to focus on your goal if achieving it will make a real difference in your life.

3. **Maintainable:** How can you work on the goal on a regular basis? Provide time and develop habits so you can work on the goal every day, if possible.

Occupational Training

Learning how to do a job really well can take a lifetime. You can get off to a good start by getting the right training. Almost every job requires having basic business skills. Beyond that, many jobs require training in specific knowledge and skills. You can complete some of that training in school and some of it on the job.

Ready for a Change

At first, Adam thought he'd like working at the convenience store. The job was pretty easy and required little training. Many days, it seemed the biggest challenge was keeping the coffee pots full. Adam didn't have any responsibilities or other things to worry about. He could put in his hours and go home.

But now, almost a year later, Adam hated his job. It was SO boring! He did the same things, day after day. Plus, he seemed to have no opportunities for advancement. His store manager, Willy, didn't make much more money than he did. And Willy had to work the same lousy hours that all of the store's employees did.

Adam decided he wanted to do something else. But what? He knew he was good at math, and he liked working with numbers. Looking over the total sales each day at the store was the only part of his job he found interesting.

Adam made an appointment at the community college near his home. The counselor he talked to helped him sign up for classes in math, English, and business. Taking these classes was part of the education required to become a bookkeeper. The counselor also gave Adam the phone number of a local accounting firm. After taking some classes, Adam could probably get a part-time job there. That would give him some experience and help him earn money while he went to school.

After his appointment, Adam thought the future looked more interesting already.

Chapter 1

Basic Business Skills

Before building a house, a contractor puts down a ***foundation.***
Before you go to work in the business world, you should put down
a foundation, too. That
foundation should be made
up of the skills needed to read,
to do math, to speak well,
and to perform basic tasks on
a computer.

Foundation

The structure or base that
supports something.

Communication Skills

You'll need to read and understand many things when you're on the job. For instance, you might need to read and write memos. *Memos* are informal notes that employees write to one another or that supervisors write to their employees. A memo may give instructions or tell about a meeting that's coming up. Or perhaps you'll read formal business letters from customers or suppliers or exchange e-mails with them.

If you don't understand a memo, letter, or e-mail, you won't be able to do what needs to be done. And if you don't know how to use a computer, you won't be able to write and send any of these pieces of written communication.

Speaking well is another important job skill. *All* jobs require that you communicate. You might need to describe products and services or to set up appointments for people. And you must be able to speak confidently at workplace meetings.

Tips for Becoming a Better Speaker

1. **Model good speakers.** Pay attention to people you think are good speakers. How do they change the tone and volume of their voice? How do they use their hands?

2. **Connect with the topic.** Try to find a personal connection to the topic you're speaking about. Doing so will help put you at ease and make you more convincing.

3. **Practice.** Look for opportunities to speak in front of others. For instance, offer to read aloud in class or to introduce someone at a meeting.

4. **Take a course or join a group.** Find a course in public speaking at your local community college. Also look for a group such as Toastmasters, which provides practice and feedback.

Employability Skills

Many surveys of employers have produced lists of what they look for in employees. Of course, most employers require specific knowledge and skills in the people they hire. But employers also look for *employability skills*. These skills are general

personal qualities that have been shown to make someone a good employee. Of all these skills, what's the one employers almost always list as most important? Communication skills. Being able to listen, write, and speak well is important in every job.

Computer and Math Skills

Think Math

Most jobs have forms that must be filled out or created on a computer. You may even need to read and understand a contract or a legal agreement about your work. Invoices and purchase orders are common in the business world. These forms *document* the costs of things that people buy and sell.

Do you think a calculator or computer can do all of your business math? It's true that these tools are a great help. But you'll also need to be able to "think math." Do you understand how to compare prices? Can you figure out measurements, such as distances and weights?

On the job, you may need to understand percentages, such as *commissions.* Suppose you are a motorcycle salesperson and make a lot of sales in April. Your commission will be a percentage of all your sales that month. To make sure you get paid the right amount, you'll need to figure out what your commission is supposed to be.

Having a working understanding of computers is necessary in almost every line of work. So is having strong skills in speaking, reading, and basic math.

Document
To record or provide evidence of something.

Commission
A percentage of the total amount of sales.

[FACT]

Social Skills and Job Success

Many people would probably say that being intelligent is the key to doing well on the job. But as it turns out, having good social skills is more important. Social skills include getting along with others, communicating clearly, being self-confident, and so on. Research on job success has proven that having good social skills is about twice as important as being smart. This finding has held true for all kinds of jobs in all kinds of businesses. People with good social skills even earn more over a lifetime, on average.

CHAPTER 2

Occupational Training

Jay is a skilled guitar player. His rock band gets hired to play at local events every once in a while. He loves performing and looks forward to earning more money as a musician.

Jay's dad is very proud of his son's accomplishments. But he warns Jay that he needs a **reliable** source of income. "You need to find a career you can depend on for a steady paycheck," he tells his son. "You need a **vocation**."

Choosing a Vocation

Jay doesn't know how to find a vocation. So, he mentioned his problem to his uncle, Cody. Cody is an EMT (emergency medical technician). He learned how to do this job by taking courses at the local community college. Cody told Jay about the special training he received. He also admitted that he's thrilled to be able to save people's lives.

Cody's best friend, Eduardo, took auto shop classes in high school. Then, he went on to learn engine rebuilding at a nearby *vo-tech.* Now, Eduardo is a mechanic at Al's Auto Clinic. Eduardo's girlfriend, Angie, is a hairstylist. She learned her vocation at a private *academy* she found advertised on TV.

Reliable
Dependable and consistent.

Vocation
A career or profession. In general use, someone's *vocation* is what he or she does as a job.

Vo-tech
Stands for *vocational-technical.* This is a type of school that offers courses in the trades, such as being an electrician or machinist.

Academy
A school that specializes in one area or program.

After talking to all these people, Jay is beginning to get the picture. He realizes that even Jamal—who used to be his band's back-up drummer—has a vocation. Jamal had always liked the idea of driving big rigs. Using the online Yellow Pages, he found the name and phone number of a training school for truck drivers. He used his savings to learn how to drive an 18-wheeler. Now, he's a long-haul driver, moving freight between Kansas City and Chicago.

Getting the Right Education and Training

Most vocations require a high school diploma, so graduating is Jay's first step. At his high school, he talks to a guidance counselor about vocational opportunities. He finds

out that the local school system works closely with area businesses. Together, they offer many vocational classes for jobs such as veterinary assistant, office management, computer repair, Web design, graphics technology, retail merchandising (selling), video production—even medical jobs.

Jay will consider all of his choices and target the career that suits him best. Now, he has two goals: to be a top guitarist and to learn how to do an interesting job that provides a steady paycheck.

Choosing a Vo-Tech

- **Program:** Does the vo-tech offer the program you're interested in?

- **Location:** Is the school nearby or in an area you're willing to move to?

- **Flexibility:** Will the program fit in with your job, family, or other responsibilities?

- **Faculty:** What qualifications and experience do the teachers at this school have?

- **Job placement:** Will attending this school help you get a job after you complete the program?

- **Cost:** How much will it cost you to complete a program at this school? Are scholarships or financial aid available?

Business Colleges

Business colleges provide another option for postsecondary education. (*Postsecondary* means beyond high school.) In the past, these colleges offered courses only in bookkeeping, and typing/word processing. The courses were intended for people planning to work as assistants in an office setting. Most business colleges awarded two-year degrees called *associate's degrees.* Today, most business colleges offer many more kinds of courses. And some offer four-year degrees called *bachelor's degrees.* Programs may be available in jobs ranging from lab technician to hair stylist to recording engineer.

Chapter 3

Community College

Exploring Options

Maya and Sean have been friends since their freshman year in high school. Now that they're almost ready to graduate, they've been talking about what they want to do. Maya is planning a career in nursing. She's pretty well set with her plans. Sean wants to be a police officer. But he's puzzled about the fastest way to get into the police academy.

"My cousin Ed is a cop," Sean explained to Maya. "He told me to join the army and get into the military police. He said that when I get out, I can move right into a police job. But being in the army will take three years. I'll be an old man by then!"

Maya laughed. She knew a quicker way for Sean to get into the police academy.

Going to a Community College

Sean could go with Maya to the two-year community college. She was going there to take classes in medical terminology and laboratory work. Her lab class was teaching her how to take blood samples from patients. Taking it would qualify her to work as a medical assistant. The wages she'd earn at a medical clinic would help pay her *tuition* to nursing school.

Tuition
The fee a student pays to take classes at a school.

Maya showed Sean the college catalog. This book listed all the classes the college offered. Included in the catalog were classes in criminal justice for students interested in police work.

"Look, there's a class called Law Enforcement Skills," Maya told Sean. "That will help connect you to the police reserve. You can get work experience."

Maya went on to explain that the cost of attending a community college was much lower than that of a four-year university. There were other benefits, too. Community colleges do much more than prepare students for jobs. They offer all the regular academic courses, such as math, history, biology, English, and economics.

After earning an associate of arts (AA) degree, many students *transfer* to a four-year university. There, they earn a four-year bachelor of arts (BA) or bachelor of science (BS) degree. That's what Maya will have to do to become a registered nurse (RN).

Transfer

To move from one college or university to another. Usually, students transfer from a two-year college to a four-year university. The courses they complete at the college usually count toward the degree they will earn at the university.

Maya was right. By taking *general education* courses at the community college, she and Sean could get their AA degrees, plus valuable job training. That would give them much better *qualifications* to move on to better jobs. And they could develop their other interests, too. The community college also offered classes in drama, art, gardening, chorus, and creative writing. There was something useful or fun for everyone, it seemed!

General education

Courses in math, English, science, and other general subjects that are required to get a college degree. These courses are intended to provide a broad base of knowledge.

Qualifications

The knowledge, skills, or other qualities that make someone able to do a particular job.

Benefits of Attending a Community College

- **Cost:** Tuition at community colleges is usually lower than at four-year universities.

- **Admission:** Community colleges almost always have an open admissions policy. That means that anyone with a high school diploma or GED is allowed to attend.

- **Convenience:** Community colleges tend to offer courses at several different times. Classes may be available during the day, at night, and even on weekends. Having options for different times fits the schedules of students with jobs or families.

- **Degree programs:** Most programs at community colleges result in getting a two-year degree or a professional certificate. Many students from community colleges transfer to four-year universities.

Drawbacks of Attending a Community College

- **Transferring:** The course credits earned at a community college aren't always accepted at a four-year university. Students who transfer might have to take some classes over again.

- **Sports and other "extras":** Most community colleges don't have sports teams, student clubs, and other extras found at universities. The reason for this is that most students at these colleges don't live at or near the college.

CHAPTER **4**

On-the-Job Training

Training in the Trades

Erica has many interests, but her
first love has always been building
things. She was pretty sure she'd
like construction work, but she
didn't know how to get started.

Her woodshop teacher said,
"Go downtown to the carpenters'

union office. They have a program for ***apprentices.*** They'll train you and put you to work with an experienced carpenter. And since it's union work, you'll be getting good pay, health insurance, and other great benefits while you learn."

Erica's friend Kyle went with her to check it out. The carpenters' union was in the same building as the Central Labor Council. There, Kyle learned about union programs for apprentices in many other trades as well: plumbing, plastering, roofing, welding, sheet metal work, and more. The apprentices in each program attended classes, and they were trained on the job by skilled workers called ***journeymen.***

Union

An organization of workers. The organization is formed to protect workers' common goals and to improve their working conditions.

Apprentice

Someone who is learning a trade by working under a skilled and experienced supervisor. Most apprentices must work in this position for two or more years.

Journeyman

Someone who has completed an apprenticeship and is certified or licensed to work as an assistant or employee. A journeyman usually works under a master tradesman or other more experienced supervisor.

The secretary of the Central Labor Council told Kyle and Erica to look online or in the phone book for the term "Labor Organizations." They found additional information on the Internet. For example, they discovered that almost all of the programs had an educational requirement. An apprentice candidate had to have a high school diploma or have passed the test for a GED. (Remember that a GED is the equivalent of a high school diploma.)

After passing entry-level tests, Erica went into the carpentry program and Kyle became a plumber's apprentice. Both liked the fact that they were earning wages while they learned their jobs. Earning money made them feel capable and independent.

What Trades Have Journeymen?

- **Electricity:** Some journeymen install and repair electrical systems in homes and office buildings. Individuals called *linemen* work on power lines.

- **Plumbing:** Journeymen in this trade install or repair pipes and fixtures in homes and offices. They may also lay sewer, water, and gas lines.

- **Construction:** Many construction journeymen do carpentry and build homes and offices. Others are ironworkers, who construct frameworks for buildings, bridges, and tunnels.

- **Vehicle repair:** These journeymen often specialize in making detailed repairs on different kinds of vehicles: cars, boats, industrial equipment, and diesel engines.

Having an Internship

The school guidance counselor told Erica's sister, Kelly, about another kind of supervised training program called an **internship.** Internships were available for many different kinds of jobs, such as computer programming, landscaping, and veterinary assistance.

Kelly was an animal lover. So, she was excited about getting an internship with a veterinarian. She was eager to learn how to take care of all kinds of sick and injured animals. Soon, she was taking vo-tech

Internship

A job done by someone with basic skills and experience in a field he or she would like to work in. The job may or may not be a paid position.

courses every morning and getting on-the-job training at a veterinary hospital every afternoon.

Both apprenticeships and internship programs offer a clear path toward career success. Combining education and training is one of the best ways to get started.

Finding an Internship

The competition for internships is usually tough. Many college students, especially, want internships for their summer jobs. To find an internship, be sure to explore all your options. Check with the following people and places:

- Career services office at your college or university
- Department office or faculty of your college major or minor
- Job and career fairs
- Friends, family, professors, and co-workers
- Alumni office at your college or university
- Web sites of companies you're interested in

Applying for a Job

Today, more than ever, there are many places to look for jobs. You might look in the newspaper or online. Or you might talk to someone at an employment agency. There are also several ways to apply for jobs. You might apply in person or submit your application materials using e-mail. In any case, you'll be more successful if you know what employers are looking for.

Using All of Your Resources

Mai had heard in the news that young people were having trouble finding jobs. Most them didn't have a lot of work experience. But employers wanted to hire experienced workers.

Mai didn't have a lot of work experience, either. But she was a good student and had won several awards during high school. She'd also done volunteer work at a food bank. Mostly, she'd answered the phone and updated records on the computer. She'd also helped with the organization's annual fundraiser. Through that event, she'd met a few people in the local business community.

Mai thought about how to get a job based on her success as a student and a volunteer. Some kind of office job seemed a good

fit. She had excellent computer skills. And she liked talking to people on the phone and in person. Maybe she could get a job as a receptionist or administrative assistant.

Mai started looking for these kinds of jobs. She checked out ads in the newspaper and online. And even though it was hard to do, she called some of the business people she'd met at the food bank's fundraiser. One of them invited her to come in for an interview!

Mai knew that she might not get the job. Lots of people were looking for work! But as she typed up her résumé, she felt she had a good chance. She was certain she had a lot to offer.

CHAPTER **1**

Job Search Resources

Online Resources

Internet job boards, Web sites, and search engines are excellent places to look for jobs. See what comes up when you enter "Jobs" in a search engine. Most Web sites will let you narrow your search.

Resources
Things that provide information or advice about a particular topic.

The Web site www.usajobs.gov lists only jobs available with the US government. Other sites allow you to search for jobs all over the world. You can usually apply for these jobs online.

Applying for Jobs Online

Job listings and application materials can be found on many companies' Web Sites. Look for a section called "Job Openings" or "Employment."

Most Popular Web Sites for Jobs

1. Yahoo! HotJobs
2. Careerbuilder
3. Monster
4. Indeed
5. Simplyhired
6. AOL jobs
7. Snagajob
8. USAJobs
9. Jobs
10. The Ladders

How can you make sure your online application is complete and correct?

→ Follow directions carefully. Enter the correct information in the correct fields, which are the spaces provided.

→ Complete all the fields on the application, even if they're not required.

→ Use fields labeled "Comments" and "Other Information" to add information the application doesn't ask for. In particular, provide details about your skills and what you've found out about the company.

→ Don't just cut-and-paste information from your résumé into the application. Tailor the information for the position and the company.

→ Use terms commonly used in the field you're applying in. Doing so shows that you're familiar with current products and practices.

→ If possible, run a spell-check and a grammar-check on the information you type in.

Understanding the Language Used in Classifieds

Classified ads are another great place to search for a job, whether online or in the newspaper. Look under a heading such as "Employment," "Help Wanted," or something similar.

Classified ads are usually full of ***abbreviations.*** Most ads use the same or similar abbreviations. For example, *req.* or *reqd.* means "required." See the chart on the next page to find out what other abbreviations mean. If you learn what the abbreviations mean, you'll be able to make sense of the ads. If you can't figure out what an abbreviation means, call the newspaper's classified ads department or search online.

You should also learn what certain terms and expressions mean. For example, "No phone calls" means you must apply in person. What

Classified

Describes a system for organizing information by types or classes. Job ads in newspapers and online are *classified* because they're organized by types of jobs.

Alphabetical

Describes a system for organizing information by the letters of the alphabet. For instance, items or names that that begin with A come first, followed by those that begin with B.

Abbreviation

A shortened form of a word or phrase used in place of the whole thing. For example, the word *ad* is an abbreviation for *advertisement*.

about an ad that wants someone who can "multitask"? That employer is looking for a person who can handle several responsibilities at the same time.

Like most classified ads, the ones below are listed in *alphabetical* order. Do any of these listings interest you?

HELP WANTED

BAKERY Counter positions avail. PT only. Looking for energetic, happy people to sell good things to eat. Apply 120 Basin St. No phone calls.

COUNTER HELP For fast-paced dry cleaners. PT. No exp reqd. Will train. Call 777-7777.

CUSTODIAN FT. $12.00 p/h. HS dip or GED. Refs reqd. Apply TBR Unified School District, 1765 Hwy 2, Greenville.

CUSTOMER SERVICE Leading kennel seeks fun, friendly animal lover for PT flex work. Avail weekends. Exp pref. Fax résumé 555-5555 or e-mail judy@kennel.com.

DRIVER/WAREHOUSE WORK M-F. FT/PT. Must be able to lift 75 lbs. Bring clean DMV printout to 111 Eli Street.

OFFICE ASST/AUTO SHOP FT. $1,500/mo. Must be good communicator, able to multitask, self-motivated. Call Jeff ASAP at 444-4444.

RESTAURANT COOKS. Exp req. FT/PT. Day/night. Refs req. Must be dependable, great attitude, and be a team player. Apply in person at Cathy's Cafe, 606 B Street.

SALES ASSOCIATE FT/PT. Exp pref. HS dip. Must be friendly and outgoing. Apply in person at Fifth Street Fashions, 1622 Fifth St.

WAREHOUSE PT nights. M-F. 30 hrs. $12 p/h. No exp req. Refs req. Apply ASAP. Call Hank at 555-1533.

[FACT]

Abbreviations Used in Classified Ads

FT = Full time

PT = Part time

FT/PT = Full time or part time

20 hrs = 20 hours a week

$10 p/h = $10 per hour

$2,000/mo = $2,000 per month

Sal = Salary

M-F = Monday through Friday

Exp = Experience

Req = Required

Pref = Preferred

Flex = Flexible

Avail = Available

Refs = References

HS dip = High school diploma

GED = General Educational
    Development certificate

ASAP = As soon as possible

Tips for Job Hunting with Classified Ads

- Answer an ad when it first appears or just before the closing date. Either way, your application will be near the top of the pile.

- Make sure to get your application in before the closing date. If it's late, it might be thrown out.

- Apply for jobs for which you have 50% of the requirements. Many ads are employers' "wish lists." Employers may not expect to find someone with all the qualities listed.

- Keep careful records of all the jobs you apply for. It sometimes takes weeks for an employer to fill a job.

- If you send in application materials, make sure they are prepared neatly and are free of errors.

- Beware of ads that make big promises about "dream jobs." If a job sounds too good to be true, it probably is.

- Avoid so-called blind ads. They don't name the company and often have a PO box for an address. In many cases, these ads are placed by employment or sales agencies—not companies with job openings.

- Don't limit yourself to the want ads when looking for work. As few as 1 in 10 jobs is filled through these ads. Also call and visit companies to look into jobs.

Chapter 2

Agencies: Private and State

Choosing an Employment Agency

Mario couldn't find a good job in the classified ads or on any Web sites. So, he looked up "Employment Agencies" in the online Yellow Pages. He was surprised at how many there were in his area.

Several agencies **specialized** in listing full-time professional, financial, or administrative jobs. Another agency focused on jobs in construction and other trades. And a few agencies offered temporary jobs, which is what Mario wanted. Some of these temporary assignments even provided benefits, such as health insurance and paid vacation time.

Mario picked one of the temporary agencies and made an appointment to go in. He thought

Agency
An organization or business that provides a service for another organization or business.

Specialize
To focus on and become good at.

Types of Employment Agencies

1. **Employment placement agencies** list regular job openings and place people in permanent jobs.

2. **Temporary help or temporary staffing agencies** put people in jobs for a limited time. Many of these jobs are seasonal or last only through a company's busy period.

3. **Executive search services** find jobs for people with specific managerial and leadership skills. These services are sometimes called *recruiters* or *headhunters*.

4. **Professional employment organizations** provide human resources services. They basically hire and manage employees for other businesses.

he might have to pay a fee to use this service, but it was free of charge. Employers of various companies paid the temporary agency to find dependable workers for them.

First, Mario was thoroughly **evaluated**. His interview included an aptitude test and a personal history check. After discussing the results, Mario and the agency worker agreed that he would be best at office tasks.

One of the forms Mario filled out became his *résumé*. A résumé is a brief summary of someone's personal, educational, and professional information. The next day, Mario got his first job interview and was hired within several

Evaluate

To examine and judge.

hours' time! In his new job, he would be working in the mailroom of a nearby business.

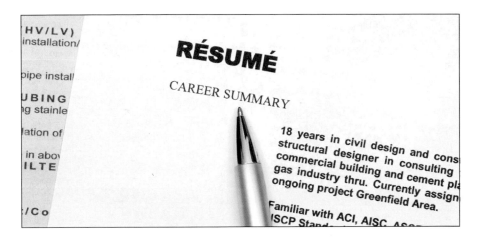

State Employment Departments

Mario's neighbor, Susan, got job help from a different kind of agency. She contacted her state's Department of Employment. On its Web site, the department offered a long list of jobs and job descriptions. Free to the public, the job search program was available at career centers all around the state. At these centers, users could search for local, state, and national jobs.

The program also offered easy-to-use forms for creating an electronic résumé. This form of résumé can be e-mailed to employers. Making a résumé was as simple as answering the questions the computer asked. Susan was

State Employment Web Sites

Each state has a Web site for its employment agency. In addition to listing job openings, these sites often provide information about the following:

- Job training
- Issues facing specific groups of workers, such as veterans and youth
- Safety and health regulations
- Hiring and salaries
- Unemployment and workers' compensation
- Discrimination
- Career planning
- Job fairs

able to make an instant document about her work experience and interests. Then, after she found a good job listing, she e-mailed her new résumé to that employer.

Susan knew other job seekers who lived miles from a career center but used the state agency to help them find jobs, too. They used their home computers or computers at the local library to search the online job listings and e-mail résumés.

Reasons for Doing Temp Work

1. **To earn money:** Many people do temporary jobs while they look for work in their desired career. Others take temp jobs while working at another job or going to school.

2. **To get work experience:** Working a temporary job is an excellent way to learn new skills or to polish existing ones. Working temp jobs also helps avoid having time gaps between jobs on your résumé.

3. **To "get a foot in the door":** In some cases, a temporary job can lead to a permanent one. Working a temp job also provides an opportunity to network and make valuable connections.

4. **To try out new careers:** Doing temp work is an ideal way to sample new careers.

Chapter 3

Résumés and Cover Letters

Creating a Résumé

A *résumé* is a summary of your personal information, education, and work experience. It should be no more than two pages long. Many employers prefer résumés that are just one page long.

Start with basic personal facts about yourself: your name, home address, phone number, and e-mail address, if you have one. Then, write a short paragraph about what kind of career you're interested in. Next, mention your job skills and **desirable** personal qualities, such as reliability, **punctuality,** and **eagerness** to learn.

Desirable	**Punctuality**	**Eagerness**
Popular or attractive.	The habit of arriving on time or completing work on time.	Excitement or enthusiasm.

Also briefly describe your education, training, and work experience. List the jobs you've had. Include the company name, when you worked there, and what you did. Focus on what you did best and enjoyed most. And if you've done volunteer work, mention it, too. Next, list the schools you've attended. Include when you attended them and what diplomas or degrees you earned. Make note of any awards or honors you received.

Finally, mention that you will provide the names of references upon request. Don't include that information in your résumé, however.

Tips for Writing Résumés

1. **Use key words:** Use the words that appear in the description of the job, such as *qualifications* and *efficient*. Also use the words commonly used in the field or business.

2. **Be concise:** Keep in mind that a résumé is scanned, not read from top to bottom. Make your résumé easy to scan by being brief. Include only important information.

3. **Use numbers:** Highlight what you've achieved by using numbers. For instance, state that you "Raised $50,000 in donations." This statement is much more powerful than "Was a successful fundraiser."

Mary Garcia

312 Sterling Road, Irvine, CA 92618   (949) 555-2345

OBJECTIVE: A customer service position, preferably in the educational book industry field.

SKILLS:
- excellent organizational skills
- computer proficiency (Powerpoint, Microsoft Office, Microsoft Word, Excel)
- word processing & typing
- data entry

EXPERIENCE: Customer Service Supervisor

Fearon Education, Belmont, CA

Performed both order processing and customer service duties on the phone and through the email, as well as computer data entry and inventory control responsibilities. Supervised a staff of 12.

Customer Service Clerk

Fox Manufacturing, Redwood City, CA

EDUCATION: Word Processing/Spreadsheets

San Mateo Community College

Diploma: Sequoia High School, Belmont

REFERENCES: Furnished on request.

Creating a Cover Letter

Along with your résumé, you'll send a *cover letter*. This letter states your interest in the job. It also tells the employer why you're the ideal person for that job. Your cover letter should be no more than one full page.

In writing the letter, emphasize the facts about you that connect with the requirements stated in the job description. For example, if the description asks for someone who's willing to work flexible hours, mention that you are agreeable to having flexible hours. You might even say that you *prefer* working flexible hours because you go to school on weekdays. Your goal in writing your cover letter is to persuade the employer to look at your résumé and call you for an interview.

Both the résumé and cover letter should be neatly typed on good-quality paper. Double-check your spelling and grammar for accuracy. Sign the letter. And make sure you address the letter and the envelope to the right person!

312 Sterling Road
Irvine, CA 92618
July 25, 2011

Ms. Jennifer Smith
Saddleback Educational Publishing
3120 Pullman Street
Costa Mesa, CA 92626

Dear Ms. Smith:

I'm writing in response to your advertisement for a position in your customer service department.

I have six years of customer service experience, the last three of which was in the educational book publishing and sales industry. My previous employer was acquired by an East Coast company and moved their location.

I have found working in the field of educational book sales to be very rewarding and would appreciate the opportunity to discuss with you how my skills and experience might benefit your company.

If after reviewing my attached résumé you would like to meet, I can be reached at 555-2345.

Sincerely,

Mary Garcia

Mary Garcia

Tips for Writing Cover Letters

- Address your letter to a specific person, if possible.
- Show your personality without seeming silly or odd.
- Be brief. Provide only relevant, useful information.
- Give specific examples of your best work.
- Follow instructions for what information to include.
- Provide your contact information.
- Review your writing, and fix any spelling and grammar mistakes.
- Avoid sounding desperate or negative.
- Show that you know something about the company.
- Sign the letter!

Things NOT to Mention in Your Résumé or Cover Letter

- Bad grades or negative work experiences
- Criticisms of your current or former employer
- Personal hobbies or interests (unless related to the job)
- A photograph or description of appearance (unless related to the job)
- Personal health or disabilities
- Membership in unions or political parties
- Whether you are married or have children
- Religious beliefs
- Jokes or other humor
- Current or expected salary (unless asked for this information)

CHAPTER **4**

Completing a Job Application

When you apply for a job, you'll be asked to complete a job *application*. It's a simple form employers use to gather information about you. A **typical** application looks like the one shown on page 84.

Typical
Usual or regular.

Information Requested

The first part of a job application usually asks for personal information. You'll be asked to provide your name, address, phone number, and Social Security number.

A job application usually asks for education and work experience, too. For each job you list, you'll be asked to provide your supervisor's name and phone number. You'll also be asked to

SOCIAL SECURITY

000-000-0000

This Number Has Been Established For

state why you left the position. If you don't want the employer to contact your current or former supervisor, mention this.

Some job applications ask for references. These can include people from outside work who know you well. Put some thought into choosing three to five people. Also, let them know you're using them as references.

Most job applications also ask whether you have any criminal history. If you do, be prepared to describe it. Finally, most applications ask whether you are a US citizen and legally able to work in this country.

DESIRED EMPLOYMENT

| ARE YOU 18 YEARS OR OLDER? | PHONE |
| YES   NO | |

POSITION

| ARE YOU EMPLOYED NOW? | IF SO MAY WE INQUIRE |
| YES   NO | OF YOUR PRESENT EMPLOYER? |

EVER APPLIED TO THIS COMPANY BEFORE?
YES   NO

EVER WORKED FOR THIS COMPANY BEFORE?
YES   NO

REASON FOR LEAVING

NAME OF LAST SUPERVISOR AT T

WHO REFERRED YOU TO
E

STATE E

EDUCA
SCHOO

EMPLOYEE REFERENCE CHECK

Job Application

Personal Information

Name _____
          Last   First   Middle

Address _____
          Street   City

_____
State   Soc. Sec. # _____

Telephone _____

Position you are applying for _____

Employment History – List two most recent jobs.

Company _____ Location _____

Supervisor _____ Phone _____

Dates Worked: From _____ To _____

Reason for Leaving _____

Company _____ Location _____

Supervisor _____ Phone _____

Dates Worked: From _____ To _____

Reason for Leaving _____

Education – List two schools most recently attended.

Name and location _____ Last grade completed _____

Name and location _____ Last grade completed _____

During the last 10 years, have you ever been convicted of a crime, excluding
misdemeanors and traffic violations? _____ If yes, describe: _____

Are you legally eligible to be employed in the U.S.? _____

Your signature _____ Date _____

Filling Out the Application

In filling out a job application, be sure to put down *accurate* information. It's a good idea to review all the information before you turn in the form.

At the bottom of the application, you'll be asked to sign your name and provide the date. In doing so, you're *certifying* that the information you've given is correct, to the best of your knowledge.

Accurate
Exact and correct.

Certify
To prove or state that something is true.

Tips for Filling Out Job Applications

1. Provide all the information that's asked for.
2. Write neatly and clearly using a black or blue pen.
3. In describing your work experience, list your current or most recent job first.
4. In describing your education, list your current or most recent school first.
5. Bring along the phone numbers of the supervisors and references you plan to list.
6. If possible, bring home or download the application and practice filling it out.
7. If applying in person, dress properly.
8. Follow instructions for completing and turning in the application.
9. Review the entire application before submitting it.
10. Sign and date the application before submitting it.

"Why Are You Leaving Your Current Job?"

Good Answers

- "I'm looking for more challenging work."
- "The job is only a temporary position."
- "I can't get enough hours."
- "I don't have enough to do."
- "I'd like to switch careers."
- "I'm planning to go back to school."

Bad Answers

- "I was fired."
- "I don't get along with my boss."
- "I don't make enough money."
- "I got hurt."
- "I don't like my schedule."
- "The work is too hard."

Selecting References

- Choose people who know your strengths and abilities.
- Choose people who will say positive things about you.
- Select people with whom you have current or recent contact.
- Pick a variety of people who will provide different information about you.
- Choose people whom employers will be able to reach easily.
- If you have previous work experience, select supervisors or co-workers.
- If you are a student, select teachers, coaches, or advisors.
- Avoid listing family members and personal friends.

The Job Interview

Most people are nervous about job interviews. They're not sure of what to say and what to ask. They worry about what to wear and how to act. You can avoid these worries by learning some basic skills for job interviews. Knowing how to have a good interview will make you more confident. And being confident is one of the keys to getting the job!

Planning for Success

Connor was feeling pretty happy with himself. He'd just had an interview for a job at a landscaping company and it had gone really well! He felt good about his chance of getting the job.

Having a good interview didn't happen by chance. Connor had prepared for it. In fact, he'd started getting ready several days before the interview.

First, Connor looked up Green Acres Landscaping online. He found out how the company got started and what kinds of work it did. Knowing this information helped Connor think of some questions to ask during the interview. It also gave him an idea of the questions he would have to answer.

The night before the interview, Connor planned what he would wear. He decided to wear dress pants and a shirt and tie. He knew that's not what workers at a landscaping business would wear. But he wanted to show he was serious about the interview and the job.

The next morning, Connor arrived at Green Acres a few minutes before his scheduled interview time. He didn't want to be late! When he met Mr. Jackson, the owner, he shook hands. He also smiled and looked the owner squarely in the eye. Throughout the interview, Connor focused on Mr. Jackson. As he answered Mr. Jackson's questions, he gave specific examples of his skills and achievements.

Tomorrow morning, Connor would call Mr. Jackson. He wanted to thank the owner for the interview. He also wanted to restate his interest in working at Green Acres. Connor would do his best to persuade Mr. Jackson that he was the best person for the job!

CHAPTER 1

Businesslike Communication

When you're trying to get hired, your goal is to persuade the employer that you're the best person for the job. He or she may be interviewing many people. So, you need to make yourself stand out from all of the other *applicants.*

Applicant

Someone who's asking to be considered for a job.

Making a Good Impression

How can you make this happen? You need to make a good *impression*. Here are some ways to do that:

→ **When you call to ask about a job, speak clearly.** Don't talk so fast that this person can't figure out what you're saying. And don't talk so softly that he or she can't hear you. If you leave a voicemail message, clearly state your whole name. If you have an unusual name, spell it. Then, give your telephone number, one number at a time. Suggest a good time to call you back. You might say, "I can be reached between 9:00 a.m. and noon," and then give your number.

→ **When you're having an interview, sit or stand up straight.** Also be sure to look the person in the eye when listening or speaking to him or her. Employers are looking for someone with *confidence* and who's comfortable with other people.

Impression

A general feeling or belief. The *impression* you make on someone is what he or she remembers most about you.

Confidence

The sense of believing in one's own abilities.

→ **When responding to an ad, give all of the information requested.** And be sure to read over what you've written before you send anything. Use a dictionary or computer spell-check program to make sure your spelling is correct. Also, tell the employer the best way to contact you, and provide this information. Sign your full name.

....

Signature

→ **If you're mailing or dropping off an application, make sure it looks as neat as possible.** Look over the application. Is the paper clean? Are there any mistakes? If you find a mistake, don't cross it out. Get another piece of paper or another form, and do it over again.

→ **Make copies of everything.** It's important to keep copies of all the paperwork you send out. You may need to talk about these materials with the employer. Or you may want to use them again when you're applying for another job.

Making Eye Contact

One of the best and easiest ways to create a good impression is to make eye contact. Looking people in the eye tells them that

you're comfortable talking to them. It shows that you're confident. Making eye contact also tells people that you're interested and paying attention. Finally, it tells them that you're open and honest.

Not making eye contact suggests all the opposites. It makes people think that you're nervous and worried. It might also make them think that you're not interested in what they have to say. People might even think that you have something to hide.

The Basics of Body Language

A lot of what we communicate comes through our bodies, not our words. Body language is the term used to label different kinds of nonverbal or unspoken communication:

Body Language	Positive Communicationr	Negative Communication
Posture	Standing or sitting up straight shows you are interested and confident.	Slouching suggests you are distracted and unsure of yourself.
Hands	Gesturing naturally while you speak shows energy and confidence.	Gesturing wildly or inconsistently suggests you are nervous.
Face and head	Nodding your head shows understanding and support.	Frowning suggests you don't understand or agree.
Eyes	Focusing on the speaker or item being discussed shows you are paying attention.	Looking away suggests you are uninterested.
Mouth	Smiling naturally shows warmth and excitement.	Not smiling suggests worry or concern. Smiling unnaturally suggests dishonesty or nervousness.

Applying for Jobs Online

Many companies allow you to complete a job application online. Others allow you to e-mail your résumé and cover letter. Before doing either, take some time to get organized:

- Get your own e-mail address. Several free e-mail services are available, such as Gmail and Hotmail.

- Make sure you have regular Internet access. If you don't have a computer at home, you might be able to use one at a local library.

- Save your résumé and cover letter in two file formats. Save both as Word files and PDF files. These are the file types employers usually want from people applying online.

CHAPTER **2**

Dressing for Success

You're getting ready for your first job interview! What will you wear?

The image you ***project*** is

Project
To give off or create.

important. You want the interviewer to see that you care about yourself. That will indicate that you care about other things, too. Dressing poorly will definitely work against you.

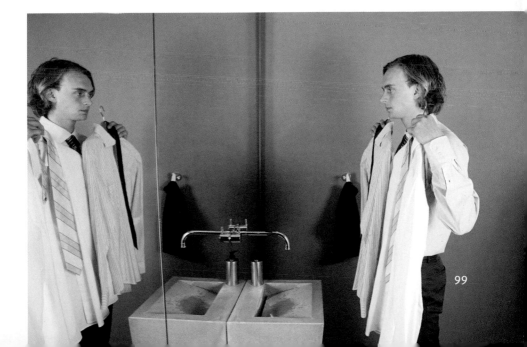

Play It Smart!

→ **Get organized.** Decide ahead of time what you'll wear to the interview. Choose clothes that are right for the season and the weather. Also, choose clothes that are right for the job you're applying for. But for every interview, you should dress as professionally as possible.

→ **Check yourself out.** Try on your outfit and look yourself over. Are your clothes clean and pressed? Do they have any tears or missing buttons? Is your outfit well *coordinated?* Do the colors match

99

or look good together? For example, a light-blue shirt or blouse goes well with a skirt or pants that are gray, black, or dark blue.

Coordinated
Designed to look good or work well together.

→ **Be serious.** Ask yourself this question: "Do I want people to pay more attention to my clothes or to *me*?" Don't wear outfits that are too flashy or *revealing.* Your interviewer may look at your clothes instead of paying attention to you. Also avoid looking like you're dressed up for a party. The interviewer might not think you're serious about getting the job.

Revealing
Showing too much of the body. *Revealing* clothing might include things that are too tight, too short or low cut, or too sheer.

→ **Less is more.** What jewelry should you wear? Don't overdo it. Again, you want to create an image that says you're serious about getting the job. A simple ring, a pair of earrings, and a watch are enough. The same goes for makeup. It's best to stick with the basics. Too much makeup can be distracting and take away from your natural look.

→ **Clean up.** The interviewer will pay attention to your ***grooming.*** Good grooming suggests care and confidence. Make sure your hair and fingernails are clean and neatly trimmed. Brush your teeth before you leave the house, and be sure that your breath is fresh.

> **Grooming**
>
> The quality of someone's personal appearance. *Grooming* can also be used to mean the process of making oneself neat and clean.

→ **Gather your paperwork.** Then think about what paperwork you need to take with you. If possible, bring along copies of all your application materials. Put them in a briefcase, folder, or envelope to protect them. Gather everything you need early, so you won't have to rush at the last minute. Being calm will make you look and feel more capable and confident.

Above all else, think positively. You're certain to have a great interview!

What to Wear to an Interview

Men

- Solid-colored suit *or* dress pants (navy, black, or dark gray)
- Long-sleeved dress shirt (white or coordinated with suit or pants)
- Belt and tie
- Dark-colored dress shoes and same-colored socks
- Little or no jewelry
- Clean, well-trimmed hair
- Clean, neatly trimmed fingernails
- Little aftershave or cologne

Women

- Solid-colored suit *or* dress pants or skirt* (navy, black, or dark gray)
- Blouse or shirt (white or coordinated with suit or pants/skirt)
- Shoes with flat or moderately high heels
- Neutral-colored pantyhose
- Little or no jewelry
- Clean, well-trimmed hair
- Light makeup and perfume
- Clean, neatly trimmed fingernails

*The skirt should be just above or below the knee.

What NOT to Bring to an Interview

- Don't chew gum or eat breath mints. Freshen your breath before the interview, not during.

- Turn off your cell phone. Don't check it at any time during the interview.

- Don't bring along your iPod or other device.

- Don't bring a cup of coffee or a bottle of water or soda into the interview.

- If you have noticeable piercings, don't wear the rings or studs. "Earrings only" is a good rule.

- If you have noticeable tattoos, cover them up.

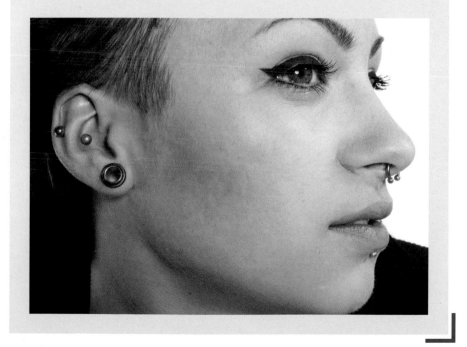

CHAPTER **3**

Answering Questions

Being interviewed for a job involves answering a lot of questions. Some of the employer's questions will be fairly simple: *How long have you lived in this area? How much did you get paid at your last job?*

Other questions will require more thought: *Why do you want this job? What are your strongest skills?*

A few questions may even be challenging: *Why should you be selected for this job? What can you contribute to this company?*

Giving Good Answers

Before answering each question, think for a moment about what you're going to say. Don't blurt out something just to start talking. Talk when you're ready. The interviewer will like the fact that you're giving your answers some thought.

If you claim to have experience at doing something, be able to back it up. Suppose you tell an employer you can drive an 18-wheeler. Then you'd better have a trucker's license to prove your experience. Likewise, if you say you've made deliveries in a large city, be able to describe the locations you've visited. Or if you say you've been successful working with children, give some specific examples.

Also be willing to give the interviewer some references to call. Provide the names of people who will describe you as a hard-working, *competent* employee.

Competent

Having the necessary skills or knowledge. Being able to do something.

Asking Your Own Questions

At the *conclusion* of the interview, you may be invited to ask your own questions. You might ask the date the employer would want you

to start. Or if you don't know the exact salary, you might ask about it. You might say something like, "I'm not quite sure about the hourly wage. Can you *clarify* that for me?"

Conclusion
The final or closing part of something.

Clarify
To make clear.

Questions to Ask in a Job Interview

- What responsibilities would I have in this position?
- What is a typical day or week like in this job?
- How many people work at this company?
- Who would be my manager or supervisor?
- What are the possibilities for growth and advancement?
- When can I expect to hear back from you?

Ending the Interview

When the interview is over, make sure to thank the person for his or her time. Say that you **appreciate** being considered for the job. If you're sure you want the job, say that you'd be eager to accept the position.

Finally, before you leave, write down the interviewer's name or ask for his or her business card. You'll need this information to follow up later.

Appreciate

To be thankful for something or to understand its value.

Questions NOT to Ask in a Job Interview (and Why!)

- What does this company do? (Find out on your own before the interview.)

- How soon can I take vacation time? (Get the job before asking about taking time off.)

- Can I work different hours? (Again, get the job before asking for favors.)

- Will I have to work weekends or overtime? (Don't sound like you're unavailable or unwilling to work the necessary hours.)

- Do people like working here? (Avoid asking questions that ask for the interviewer's personal opinions.)

- Can you tell me now if I got the job? (Don't sound impatient or desperate.)

CHAPTER 4

The Follow-Up Call and Thank-You Letter

After you've had an interview, it's considered polite to call or write to the person who interviewed you. But which should you do? How do you decide whether it's more *appropriate* to call or write?

Appropriate

Proper or correct for the situation.

Being Pushy or Persistent?

Many job applicants aren't sure whether to follow up after an interview. They don't want to seem pushy or to bother the

interviewer. But people in the job placement business say these kinds of feelings are wrong!

The fact is, some companies wait several weeks before offering a job to anyone. They want to see which applicants do and don't follow up. They also want to see how persistent applicants are in going after something they want. Most applicants don't follow up at all. Employers see this as a sign of disinterest or a lack of professionalism.

Informal Employers

Suppose the employer is small and fairly informal. For instance, it may have just a few employees and not much of a business office. Examples might include a car wash, a coffee shop, or a limousine service.

In the case of an informal employer, it's okay to call. When you do, ask to speak to the person who interviewed you. Make sure to use the person's full name. Thank him or her for taking the time to talk with you. Also, ask if he or she has any questions you can answer. Offer to send any other information or **documents** the interviewer may want to consider. Finally, say that you appreciate being considered for the job and look forward to hearing of his or her decision.

Don't keep the interviewer on the phone a long time. Say what you need to say, and then politely end the conversation. It's always wise to offer your own telephone number again, in case it's been **misplaced**.

Documents
Formal pieces of writing, such as legal agreements.

Misplace
To lose or be unable to find.

Formal Employers

Suppose you've applied for a job at a more formal kind of business. Examples include a bank, an insurance agency, and a government office.

In these cases, it's best to write a thank-you letter to the interviewer. Your letter might look something like the one shown on page 115.

Sell Yourself!

Successful salespeople know that the most important part of selling is following up. Keep that in mind when you follow up after a job interview. Try this five-part plan:

1. At the end of the interview, get the business card of the person you talked to.

2. The night after your interview, e-mail that person. Thank him or her for taking the time to meet with you.

3. The day after the interview, send a regular-mail letter. Restate your interest in the job and the company. Summarize your skills and experience.

4. Five days after the interview, call the person. Again, restate your interest. Ask if he or she needs more information from you. Leave a short voicemail, if the person isn't available when you call.

5. Continue to call, e-mail, or send a letter once a week until you hear whether you've gotten the job.

[FACT]

Format of a Follow-Up Letter

Format your follow-up letter as a standard business letter, like the sample shown on the next page. Keep the letter short but include at least three paragraphs:

- **Paragraph 1:** Thank the person who interviewed you. State when he or she met with you. Also, mention something he or she will remember from your interview.

- **Paragraph 2:** Restate your key skills and experience. Also, mention anything important you didn't talk about in the interview.

- **Paragraph 3:** Thank the interviewer again. Offer to provide additional information, if needed. Say that you will call in a few days to follow up again.

Jeremy Snow
1212 West 18th Street
Clarkville, MN 55555
Phone: 555-818-1234
E-mail: jmsnow@mymail.com

June 5, 2011

Angela Worthington
Director of Human Relations
American Orbit Agency
1919 Main Street
Arbor Heights, MN 55545

Dear Ms. Worthington:

It was a pleasure to meet with you on June 3 to discuss the possibility of my employment at American Orbit Agency. And, of course, it's always good to meet a fellow graduate from Clark State.

I am eager to come to work for your agency. I am confident that I can use my strong computer and design skills to make a contribution as a graphic artist. I am especially skilled in adapting photographs using PhotoMaker software.

Again, I enjoyed meeting you and having the opportunity to discuss the position. I would be happy to show you some more samples of my work, if you would like to see them. I will call you later this week to follow up.

In the meantime, please call me if you require any additional information. I look forward to hearing from you.

Sincerely,

Jeremy Snow

Jeremy Snow

Word List

abbreviation
ability
academic
access
accurate
achievement
administrative
admission
advancement
agency
agreement
annual
applicant
application
appointment
appreciate
apprentice
appropriate
aptitude
assignment
assistant
attitude
attract
award

benefits
businesslike

capable
career
catalog
category
certificate
certify
challenging
checklist

chef
clarify
classified
clerical
college
commission
communication
comparison
competent
competition
concise
conditions
confident
consideration
construction
contact
contribute
convenience
coordinated
counselor
criminal
criticism

data
degree
dependable
designed
desirable
desperate
determine
device
diploma
disability
discount
discrimination
distracted

document
donation
double-check
download
drawbacks

e-mail
eager
electronic
emphasize
employment
energetic
enroll
envelope
environment
equipment
evaluation
evidence
exam
executive
expensive
experience
explanation
explore

faculty
fascinated
fee
financial
flexible
follow-up
formal
format
former
foundation
freshen

fundraiser
future

gesture
goal
graphics
grooming
guidance

hardware
heading
highlight
housing

impatient
impress
impression
income
indicate
industry
informal
install
instructions
insurance
intelligent
intend
Internet
internship
interpret
interview

laboratory
landscaping
legal
license
lifetime

Word List

loan
long-term
lousy

managerial
manufacturing
material
measurements
mechanical
medication
mention
merchandise
misplace
moderately
motivated
multitask
musician

negative
network
neutral

occupation
on-the-job
online
onsite
organized
overdo
overtime

paperwork
paragraph
particular
patience
pension
percentage

permanent
permission
persistent
personality
persuade
placement
polish
polite
position
possibilities
postsecondary
posture
preferences
preferred
preparation
presenting
process
product
profession
program
project
promote
punctuality
puzzled

qualifications
qualify
qualities

readiness
rebuilding
recommend
references
regulations
reimbursement
relevant

reliable
repair
report
request
requirements
resources
respond
response
responsibilities
restate
résumé
revealing
review

salary
satisfaction
scan
schedule
scholarship
search engine
seasonal
security
select
short-term
similarities
software
source
specialize
specific
staff
strictly
submit
summarize
supervise
sustainable

target
temporary
terminology
thrilled
time frame
trades
transfer
transportation
trim
tuition
typical

unavailable
uninterested
union
university
unnaturally
unsure
unwilling
updated

valuable
vary
variety
vehicle
veterinarian
violation
vo-tech
vocation
volunteer

wage
workplace

Index

Index

Index